Over the Hills and Far Away

Over the Hills and Far Away
A BOOK
OF NURSERY RHYMES
Selected and illustrated by
Alan Marks

A Michael Neugebauer Book
NORTH-SOUTH BOOKS / NEW YORK / LONDON

First published in the United States and Canada in 1994 by North-South Books,
an imprint of Nord-Süd Verlag AG, Gossau Zurich, Switzerland
Distributed in the United States by North-South Books Inc., New York

First published in Great Britain, Australia, and New Zealand in 1993
by Picture Book Studio Ltd., London. Reprinted in 1994 by North-South Books.

Library of Congress Cataloging-in-Publication data is available
A CIP catalogue record for this book is available from The British Library
ISBN 1-55858-285-1

Cover lettering by Julian Waters
10 9 8 7 6 5 4 3 2 1
Printed in Italy

For Elisabeth

HOW many days has my baby to play?
Saturday, Sunday, Monday,
Tuesday, Wednesday, Thursday, Friday,
Saturday, Sunday, Monday.
Hop away, skip away,
My baby wants to play every day.

HERE we go round the mulberry bush,
The mulberry bush, the mulberry bush,
Here we go round the mulberry bush,
On a cold and frosty morning.

This is the way we wash our hands,
Wash our hands, wash our hands,
This is the way we wash our hands,
On a cold and frosty morning.

This is the way we brush our hair,
Brush our hair, brush our hair,
This is the way we brush our hair,
On a cold and frosty morning.

This is the way we go to school,
Go to school, go to school,
This is the way we go to school,
On a cold and frosty morning.

This is the way we wave bye-bye,
Wave bye-bye, wave bye-bye,
This is the way we wave bye-bye,
On a cold and frosty morning.

I SAW three ships come sailing by,
Come sailing by, come sailing by,
I saw three ships come sailing by,
On New Year's Day in the morning.

And what do you think was in them then,
Was in them then, was in them then,
And what do you think was in them then,
On New Year's Day in the morning?

Three pretty girls were in them then,
In them then, in them then,
Three pretty girls were in them then,
On New Year's Day in the morning.

One could whistle, and one could sing,
And one could play the violin;
Such joy there was at my wedding,
On New Year's Day in the morning.

ONE misty moisty morning,
When cloudy was the weather,
There I met an old man
Clothed all in leather.

Clothed all in leather,
With cap under his chin,
How do you do, and how do you do,
And how do you do again!

RAIN, rain, go away,
Come again on washing day.

As I was going to St. Ives,
I met a man with seven wives;
Each wife had seven sacks,
Each sack had seven cats,
Each cat had seven kits;
Kits, cats, sacks and wives,
How many were going to St. Ives?

RIDE a cock-horse to Banbury Cross,
To see a fine lady ride on a white horse;
With rings on her fingers and bells on her toes,
She shall have music wherever she goes.

17

HOT cross buns!
Hot cross buns!
One a penny, two a penny,
Hot cross buns!

If you have no daughters,
Give them to your sons.
One a penny, two a penny,
Hot cross buns!

HAVE you seen the muffin man,
The muffin man, the muffin man?
Have you seen the muffin man
Who comes from Drury Lane?

Yes I've seen the muffin man,
The muffin man, the muffin man.
Yes I've seen the muffin man
Who comes from Drury Lane.

THIS old man, he played one,
He played knick-knack on my drum.
With a knick-knack paddy-whack give a dog a bone,
This old man came rolling home.

This old man, he played two,
He played knick-knack on my shoe.
With a knick-knack paddy-whack give a dog a bone,
This old man came rolling home.

This old man, he played three,
He played knick-knack on my knee.
With a knick-knack paddy-whack give a dog a bone,
This old man came rolling home.

This old man, he played four,
He played knick-knack on my door.
With a knick-knack paddy-whack give a dog a bone,
This old man came rolling home.

This old man, he played five,
He played knick-knack on my hive.
With a knick-knack paddy-whack give a dog a bone,
This old man came rolling home.

This old man, he played six,
He played knick-knack on my sticks.
With a knick-knack paddy-whack give a dog a bone,
This old man came rolling home.

This old man, he played seven,
He played knick-knack down in Devon.
With a knick-knack paddy-whack give a dog a bone,
This old man came rolling home.

This old man, he played eight,
He played knick-knack on my gate.
With a knick-knack paddy-whack give a dog a bone,
This old man came rolling home.

This old man, he played nine,
He played knick-knack on my line.
With a knick-knack paddy-whack give a dog a bone,
This old man came rolling home.

This old man, he played ten,
He played knick-knack on my hen.
With a knick-knack paddy-whack give a dog a bone,
This old man came rolling home.

SIMPLE SIMON met a pieman,
Going to the fair.
Said Simple Simon to the pieman,
Let me taste your ware.

Said the pieman to Simple Simon,
Show me first your penny.
Said Simple Simon to the pieman,
Sir I have not any.

Simple Simon went a-fishing
For to catch a whale.
All the water he had got
Was in his mother's pail.

Simple Simon went to look
If plums grew on a thistle.
He pricked his fingers very much,
Which made poor Simon whistle.

T HIS is the house that Jack built.

This is the malt
That lay in the house that Jack built.

This is the rat,
That ate the malt,
That lay in the house that Jack built.

This is the cat,
That killed the rat,
That ate the malt,
That lay in the house that Jack built.

This is the dog,
That worried the cat,
That killed the rat,
That ate the malt,
That lay in the house that Jack built.

This is the cow with the crumpled horn,
That tossed the dog,
That worried the cat,
That killed the rat,
That ate the malt,
That lay in the house that Jack built.

This is the maiden all forlorn,
That milked the cow with the crumpled horn,
That tossed the dog,
That worried the cat,
That killed the rat,
That ate the malt,
That lay in the house that Jack built.

This is the man all tattered and torn,
That kissed the maiden all forlorn,
That milked the cow with the crumpled horn,
That tossed the dog,
That worried the cat,
That killed the rat,
That ate the malt,
That lay in the house that Jack built.

This is the priest all shaven and shorn,
That married the man all tattered and torn,
That kissed the maiden all forlorn,
That milked the cow with the crumpled horn,
That tossed the dog,
That worried the cat,
That killed the rat,
That ate the malt,
That lay in the house that Jack built.

This is the cock that crowed in the morn,
That woke the priest all shaven and shorn,
That married the man all tattered and torn,
That kissed the maiden all forlorn,
That milked the cow with the crumpled horn,
That tossed the dog,
That worried the cat,
That killed the rat,
That ate the malt,
That lay in the house that Jack built.

This is the farmer sowing his corn,
That kept the cock that crowed in the morn,
That woke the priest all shaven and shorn,
That married the man all tattered and torn,
That kissed the maiden all forlorn,
That milked the cow with the crumpled horn,
That tossed the dog,
That worried the cat,
That killed the rat,
That ate the malt,
That lay in the house that Jack built.

I LOVE little pussy,
Her coat is so warm,
And if I don't hurt her
She'll do me no harm.
So I'll not pull her tail,
Nor drive her away,
But pussy and I
Very gently will play.
She shall sit by my side,
And I'll give her some food,
And pussy will love me
Because I am good.

ONE, two, three, four, five,
Once I caught a fish alive!
Six, seven, eight, nine, ten,
Then I let it go again.
Why did you let it go?
Because it bit my finger so.
Which finger did it bite?
This little finger on the right.

LITTLE Tommy Tittlemouse
Lived in a little house;
He caught fishes
In other men's ditches.

PETER PIPER picked a peck of pickled pepper.
A peck of pickled pepper Peter Piper picked.
If Peter Piper picked a peck of pickled pepper,
Where's the peck of pickled pepper Peter Piper picked?

PETER, PETER, pumpkin eater,
Found a wife but couldn't keep her.
He put her in a pumpkin shell,
And there he kept her very well.

Peter, Peter, pumpkin eater,
Had another and didn't love her.
Peter learned to read and spell,
And then he loved her very well.

One, two,
Buckle my shoe;
Three, four,
Knock at the door;
Five, six,
Pick up sticks;
Seven, eight,
Lay them straight;
Nine, ten,
A big fat hen;
Eleven, twelve,
Dig and delve;
Thirteen, fourteen,
Maids a-courting;
Fifteen, sixteen,
Maids in the kitchen;
Seventeen, eighteen,
Maids a-waiting;
Nineteen, twenty,
My plate's empty.

A dillar, a dollar,
A ten o'clock scholar,
What makes you come so soon?
You used to come at ten o'clock,
But now you come at noon.

LUCY Locket lost her pocket,
Kitty Fisher found it.
Not a penny was there in it,
Only ribbon round it.

LITTLE boy blue,
Come blow up your horn.
The sheep's in the meadow,
The cow's in the corn.
Where is the boy who looks after the sheep?
He's under a haycock fast asleep.
Will you wake him?
No, not I,
For if I do he's sure to cry.

ELISABETH, Elspeth, Betty and Bess,
All went together to seek a bird's nest.
They found a bird's nest with five eggs in.
They all took one and left four in.

A SWARM of bees in May
Is worth a load of hay.
A swarm of bees in June
Is worth a silver spoon.
A swarm of bees in July
Is not worth a fly.

LAVENDER'S blue, dilly, dilly,
Lavender's green.
When I am king, dilly, dilly,
You shall be queen.

Call up your men, dilly, dilly,
Set them to work,
Some to the plough, dilly, dilly,
Some to the fork.

Some to make hay, dilly, dilly,
Some to reap corn,
While you and I, dilly, dilly,
Keep ourselves warm.

ROSES are red,
Violets are blue,
Pinks are sweet,
And so are you.

WHAT are little girls made of?
Sugar and spice,
And all things nice,
That's what little girls are made of.

What are little boys made of?
Frogs and snails,
And puppy-dogs' tails,
That's what little boys are made of.

THERE was a little girl, and she had a little curl,
Right in the middle of her forehead;
When she was good she was very, very good,
But when she was bad, she was horrid!

THE Queen of Hearts,
She made some tarts,
All on a summer's day,
The Knave of Hearts,
He stole those tarts,
And took them clean away.

The King of Hearts
Called for the tarts,
And beat the knave full sore.
The Knave of Hearts
Brought back the tarts,
And vowed he'd steal no more.

TINKER,
Tailor,
Soldier,
Sailor,
Rich man,
Poor man,
Beggar man,
Thief.

SOLDIER brave,
Sailor true,
Daring airman,
Oxford blue,
Skilled physician,
Squire so hale,
Gouty nobleman,
Curate pale.

THERE was a little man,
And he had a little gun,
And his bullets were made of lead, lead, lead.
He went to the brook
And he saw a little duck,
And he shot it right through the head, head, head.

He carried it home
To his old wife Joan,
And bid her a fire for to make, make, make,
To roast the little duck
He had shot in the brook,
And he'd go and fetch her the drake, drake, drake.

TOM he was a piper's son,
He learned to play when he was young,
But all the tune that he could play
Was "Over the Hills and Far Away."
Over the hills and a great way off,
The wind shall blow my topknot off.

Now Tom with his pipe made such a noise
That he pleased both the girls and boys,
And they stopped to hear him play
"Over the Hills and Far Away."

Tom with his pipe played with such skill
That those who heard him could never keep still.
Whenever they heard they began for to dance,
Even pigs on their hind legs would after him prance.

As Dolly was milking her cow one day,
Tom took out his pipe and began for to play.
So Doll and the cow danced "The Cheshire Round,"
Till the pail was broke and the milk ran on the ground.

He met old Dame Trot with a basket of eggs,
He used his pipe and she used her legs.
She danced about till the eggs were all broke,
She began for to fret but he laughed at the joke.

Tom saw a cross fellow beating an ass,
Heavy laden with pots, pans, and glass.
He took out his pipe and played them a tune,
And the jackass's load was lightened full soon.

Over the hills and a great way off,
The wind shall blow my topknot off.

BARBER, barber, shave a pig.
How many hairs to make wig?
Four and twenty, that's enough,
Give the barber a pinch of snuff.

COBBLER, cobbler, mend my shoe,
Get it done by half past two.
Stitch it up and stitch it down,
And I will give you half a crown.

OLD Mother Hubbard

OLD Mother Hubbard
Went to the cupboard
To fetch her poor dog a bone;
But when she got there
The cupboard was bare
And so the poor dog had none.

She went to the baker's
To buy him some bread,
But when she came back
The poor dog was dead.

She went to the joiner's
To buy him a coffin,
But when she came back
The poor dog was laughing.

She took a clean dish
To get him some tripe,
But when she came back
He was smoking a pipe.

She went to the fishmonger's
To buy him some fish,
But when she came back
He was licking the dish.

She went to the ale-house
To buy him some beer,
But when she came back
The dog sat in a chair.

She went to the tavern
For white wine and red,
But when she came back
The dog stood on his head.

She went to the barber's
To buy him a wig,
But when she came back
He was dancing a jig.

She went to the hatter's
To buy him a hat,
But when she came back
He was feeding the cat.

She went to the fruiterer's
To buy him some fruit,
But when she came back
He was playing the flute.

She went to the tailor's
To buy him a coat,
But when she came back
He was riding a goat.

She went to the cobbler's
To buy him some shoes,
But when she came back
He was reading the news.

She went to the seamstress
To buy him some linen,
But when she came back
The dog was a-spinning.

She went to the hosier's
To buy him some hose,
But when she came back
He was dressed in his clothes.

The dame made a curtsy,
The dog made a bow;
The dame said, Your servant,
The dog said, Bow-wow.

A CARRION crow sat in an oak,
Watching a tailor make a cloak.
Sing heigh, sing ho, the carrion crow,
Fol de riddle, lol de riddle, hi ding do.

Wife, bring me my old bent bow,
That I may shoot yon carrion crow.
Sing heigh, sing ho, the carrion crow,
Fol de riddle, lol de riddle, hi ding do.

The tailor shot, but he missed his mark,
And shot the old sow right through the heart.
Sing heigh, sing ho, the carrion crow,
Fol de riddle, lol de riddle, hi ding do.

A WISE old owl sat in an oak.
The more he heard, the less he spoke.
The less he spoke, the more he heard.
Why aren't we all like that wise old bird?

FOUR and twenty tailors went to kill a snail.
The best man among them durst not touch her tail.
She put out her horns like a little Kyloe cow.
Run, tailors, run! Or she'll kill you all e'en now.

69

LONDON Bridge is falling down,
Falling down, falling down,
London Bridge is falling down,
My fair lady.

Build it up with wood and clay,
Wood and clay, wood and clay,
Build it up with wood and clay,
My fair lady.

Wood and clay will wash away,
Wash away, wash away,
Wood and clay will wash away,
My fair lady.

Build it up with iron and steel,
Iron and steel, iron and steel,
Build it up with iron and steel,
My fair lady.

Iron and steel will bend and bow,
Bend and bow, bend and bow,
Iron and steel will bend and bow,
My fair lady.

Build it up with silver and gold,
Silver and gold, silver and gold,
Build it up with silver and gold,
My fair lady.

Silver and gold will be stole away,
Stole away, stole away,
Silver and gold will be stole away,
My fair lady.

London Bridge is falling down,
Falling down, falling down,
London Bridge is falling down,
My fair lady.

THE lion and the unicorn
Were fighting for the crown.
The lion beat the unicorn
All around the town.

Some gave them white bread,
And some gave them brown.
Some gave them plum cake,
And drummed them out of town.

WHEN good King Arthur ruled this land,
He was a goodly king.
He stole three pecks of barley meal
To make a bag-pudding.

A bag-pudding the king did make,
And stuffed it well with plums,
And in it put great lumps of fat
As big as my two thumbs.

The king and queen did eat thereof,
And noblemen beside,
And what they did not eat that night,
The queen next morning fried.

MY dame hath a lame tame crane,
My dame hath a crane that is lame.
Please, gentle Jane, let my dame's lame tame crane
Feed and come home again.

SHE sells sea shells by the sea shore,
The shells that she sells are sea shells I'm sure.

BETTY Botter bought some butter,
But the butter, it was bitter.
If she put it in her batter,
It would make her batter bitter,
But a bit of better butter,
That would make her batter better.
So she bought some better butter,
Better than her bitter butter,
And she put it in her batter,
And the batter was not bitter.

CROSS-PATCH,
Draw the latch,
Sit by the fire and spin.
Take a cup, and drink it up,
Then call your neighbours in.

THE man in the moon
Came down too soon,
And asked his way to Norwich,
He went by the south
And burnt his mouth,
By supping on cold pease-porridge.

PEASE pudding hot,
Pease pudding cold,
Pease pudding in the pot,
Nine days old.
Some like it hot,
Some like it cold,
Some like it in the pot,
Nine days old.

LITTLE Tommy Tucker
Sings for his supper.
What shall we give him
But white bread and butter?
How shall he cut it
Without a knife?
How shall he marry
Without a wife?

DANCE to your daddy,
My little laddie,
Dance to your daddy,
My little lamb.
You shall have a fishy
On a little dishy,
You shall have a fishy
When the boat comes in.

GAY go up and gay go down,
To ring the bells of London Town.

Oranges and lemons,
Say the bells of St. Clement's.

Brickbats and tiles,
Say the bells of St. Giles'.

Bull's-eyes and targets,
Say the bells of St. Marg'ret's.

You owe me five farthings,
Say the bells of St. Martin's.

When will you pay me?
Say the bells of Old Bailey.

When I grow rich,
Say the bells of Shoreditch.

Pray, when will that be?
Say the bells of Stepney.

I'm sure I don't know,
Says the great bell of Bow.

Here comes a candle to light you to bed,
Here comes a chopper to chop off your head.

LITTLE Nancy Etticoat,
With a white petticoat
And a red nose.
She has no feet or hands,
And the longer she stands
The shorter she grows.

EARLY to bed, and early to rise,
Makes a man healthy, wealthy, and wise.

TO make your candles last for aye,
You wives and maids, give ear-o.
To put 'em out's the only way,
Says honest John Boldero.

Go to bed first,
A golden purse;
Go to bed second,
A golden pheasant;
Go to bed third,
A golden bird.

To bed, to bed!
Says Sleepyhead.
Tarry awhile, says Slow.
Put on the pan,
Says greedy Nan,
Let's sup before we go!

HUSH little baby, don't say a word,
Papa's going to buy you a mocking-bird.

If that mocking-bird won't sing,
Papa's going to buy you a diamond ring.

If that diamond ring turns to brass,
Papa's going to buy you a looking glass.

If that looking glass gets broke,
Papa's going to buy you a billy goat.

If that billy goat runs away,
Papa's going to buy you another today.

THE south wind brings wet weather,
The north wind wet and cold together.
The west wind always brings us rain,
The east wind blows it back again.

THE north wind doth blow,
And we shall have snow,
And what will the robin do then?
Poor thing!

He'll sit in a barn,
And keep himself warm,
And hide his head under his wing,
Poor thing!

NOW I lay me down to sleep,
I pray the Lord my soul to keep,
And if I die before I wake,
I pray the Lord my soul to take.

SLEEP, baby, sleep!
Thy father watches the sheep,
Thy mother is shaking the dreamland tree,
Softly a little dream falls on thee.
Sleep, baby, sleep.

Sleep, baby, sleep!
The large stars are the sheep,
The little stars are the lambs, I guess,
The fair moon is the shepherdess.
Sleep, baby, sleep.

Sleep, baby, sleep!
Thy father watches the sheep,
The wind is blowing fierce and wild,
It must not wake my little child.
Sleep, baby, sleep.